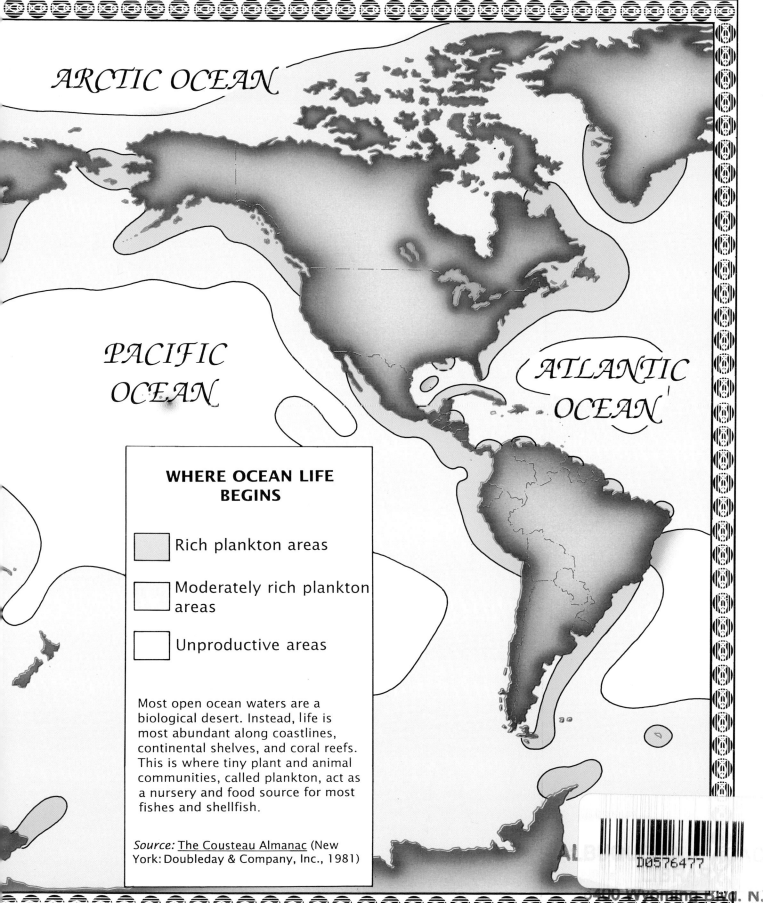

ARCTIC OCEAN

PACIFIC OCEAN

ATLANTIC OCEAN

WHERE OCEAN LIFE BEGINS

Rich plankton areas

Moderately rich plankton areas

Unproductive areas

Most open ocean waters are a biological desert. Instead, life is most abundant along coastlines, continental shelves, and coral reefs. This is where tiny plant and animal communities, called plankton, act as a nursery and food source for most fishes and shellfish.

Source: The Cousteau Almanac (New York: Doubleday & Company, Inc., 1981)

A
ALLIGATORS TO ZOOPLANKTON
Z

A DICTIONARY OF WATER BABIES

Dr. Les Kaufman
and
the Staff of the New England Aquarium

FRANKLIN WATTS
New York | London | Toronto | Sydney
A New England Aquarium Book
1991

ACKNOWLEDGMENTS

The text in this book reflects the ideas of many of us at the New England Aquarium, but we are especially indebted to Dr. Les Kaufman, former Curator of Education and now head of the Aquarium's Edgerton Research Laboratory. We wish also to thank Dr. Paul Boyle, Director of Programs and Exhibits and Acting Curator of Education, members of the education department—Terry Martin, Carol Fiore, Berit Solstad, Alan Anderson, Tanya Gregoire, and Pat Pittman—work-study student, Monica Hum, and Catherine Paladino for helping shape the answers here; and the primary writer, Ken Mallory. Finally, we would like to thank the Aquarium's Director of Marketing, Cynthia Mackey, and the Associate Director of Public Relations and Media Programs, Sandra Goldfarb, for their guiding support in making this and other books like it a reality.

Photographs copyright ©: Fred Bavendam: pp. 1, 16, 17, 18, 19, 31 top; Animals Animals: pp. 4 (C. C. Lockwood), 6, 42, 50, 51 (all Peter Parks/OSF), 7 (Colin Milkins), 12 (Robert Maier), 13 (Roger Jackman), 15 bottom (Breck P. Kent), 20 (OSF/Jim Frazier), 21 top (Oxford Scientific Films), 21 bottom (Raymond A. Mendez), 23 (Michael Fogden), 22 (OSF/Jim Clare), 35 (A. Bannister), 39 top (Steinhart Aquarium/Tom McHugh), 39 bottom (Steve Earley), 40 (George Huey), 41 (Michael Dick), 43 (OSF/G. I. Bernard), 44 (Kathie Atkinson); Roger Hanlon: pp. 8, 33 right; John Forsythe: pp. 9, 32, 33 left; T.F.H. Publications Inc.: p. 10; New England Aquarium: pp. 11, 26, 27 (both Richard Duggan), 28, 34 left (both Catherine Paladino), 30, 31 bottom, 34 right (all Kenneth Mallory), 36 (Bill Robinson), 37 (Thomas J. Coffey), 38 (Paul Erickson), 45; David Policansky: p. 15 top; Kenneth R. H. Read: p. 24; Carolina Biological Supply Company: pp. 25, 47; Photo Researchers: pp. 29; Bruce Coleman Inc.: pp. 46 (Jeff Foote), 48 (Abe Black); National Marine Fisheries Service: p. 49.

Frontispiece: Baby horseshoe crabs are almost ready to hatch out of their egg capsules.

Library of Congress Cataloging-in-Publication Data

Kaufman, Les.
  Alligators to zooplankton : a dictionary of water babies / Les Kaufman and the staff of the New England Aquarium.
    p. cm.
  "A New England Aquarium book."
  Includes bibliographical references and index.
  Summary: Describes, using a brief dictionary format, the birth and development of several aquatic species.
  ISBN 0-531-15215-4—ISBN 0-531-10995-X (lib. bdg.)
  1. Aquatic animals—Dictionaries, Juvenile. 2. Aquatic animals—Infancy—Dictionaries, Juvenile. 3. Aquatic animals—Reproduction—Dictionaries, Juvenile. [1. Aquatic animals—Dictionaries.
  2. Aquatic animals—Infancy—Dictionaries. 3. Aquatic animals—Reproduction—Dictionaries.] I. New England Aquarium Corporation.
  II. Title.
QL120.K38 1991
591.92—dc20   90-46870 CIP AC

INTRODUCTION

When it comes to caring for their young, few animals measure up to humans and other *mammals*. As you will read in the following collection of water baby stories, most aquatic parents either flood the waters with millions of sperm and eggs or they put their energies into a relatively few developing young, and then hope for the best. Between these two approaches to parental care are some of the most outrageous, inventive, and unusual stories you can find on the face of the Earth.

This book doesn't pretend to include all the stories there are to be found. Rather, think of it as a kind of field guide to animals you may someday meet. Our book also has a serious message. The more we understand the process of water baby birth, the better we can protect our threatened wildlife, and the more we will do to promote its renewal and rebirth.

American alligator *(Alligator mississippiensis)* with babies

Number of species worldwide: 2 alligators, 18 other crocodilians
Baby size: American alligator, 9 inches (23 cm) long
Adult size: American alligator, at one time to 18 feet (5.5 m), now considerably less because of hunting
Where it lives: American alligator, southeastern United States
Special features: Crocodiles and alligators are part of a family called crocodilians and the two are often confused. You can tell them apart by the shapes of their heads. The snouts of crocodiles are long and pointed, while those of alligators have much broader tips.

A
4

A

Alligator (AL-ih-gay-ter)

With a coat of horny scales, wrinkled skin, and a jaw of menacing teeth, an alligator may not be everyone's ideal of a nurturing mother. But alligator mothers take their maternal responsibilities quite seriously. First, they build complicated nests of leaves and grasses. Made in the shape of a cone, nests are sometimes 6 feet (1.8 m) wide and several feet high. Then alligator mothers bury thirty or more eggs inside an alligator's version of a compost heap.

Covered with grass and reeds, the developing eggs incubate in comfortably warm surroundings. It takes the eggs about nine weeks to develop fully. The babies break out of their shells with an "egg tooth" at the tips of their bills. Though babies ride around on their mothers' backs, and sometimes share their meals, they get most of their food (insects and other small water creatures) on their own.

Because alligators were once an endangered species, alligator farmers tried to raise them on special farms. But farmers were unsuccessful at first because they let the nests get too hot. Farmers in places like Louisiana have now learned from alligators how important it is to keep the nest temperature stable. In the wild, the sex of an alligator is determined by whether the nest is placed up on a dike, where the temperature is warm, or down near the cooler water.

B

Barnacle (BAHR-nuh-kul)

Anyone who has seen a tidepool at the seashore knows what a barnacle is. But do you know what a barnacle looks like inside its limestone house?

There are over 900 varieties of barnacles, shrimplike animals that live on their backs inside a hard shell they make for self-protection. The little feelers you see waving out of an open shell are actually barnacle feet. They trap food from the water and bring it into the animal's mouth. Some kinds of barnacle babies start life as tiny free-swimming *larva* that are carried in ocean currents. Larvae use their vision to help locate a rock or other hard surface to settle on. Then they will go through *metamorphosis* like a butterfly. The baby sticks itself to the rock with its own supply of "glue." Secure at last behind the new hard shell it has made, the barnacle is ready to begin its adult life.

One kind of barnacle is especially strange. It's a parasite called a "root head," or rhizocephalan. Its baby first attaches to a crab and then sends rootlike structures all through its victim's body. The root-head barnacle gets all the nourishment it needs from the luckless crab, which dies as a result. The barnacle remains attached to its host until it matures and produces more larvae from eggs and sperm.

Nauplius larva of gooseneck barnacle (Lepas sp.)

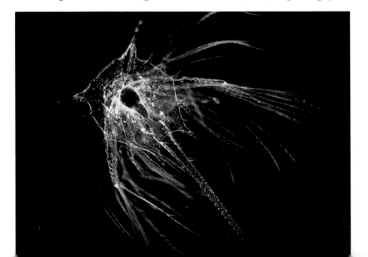

The gooseneck barnacle adult *(Lepas sp.)* **waves its feet (cirri) to catch food**

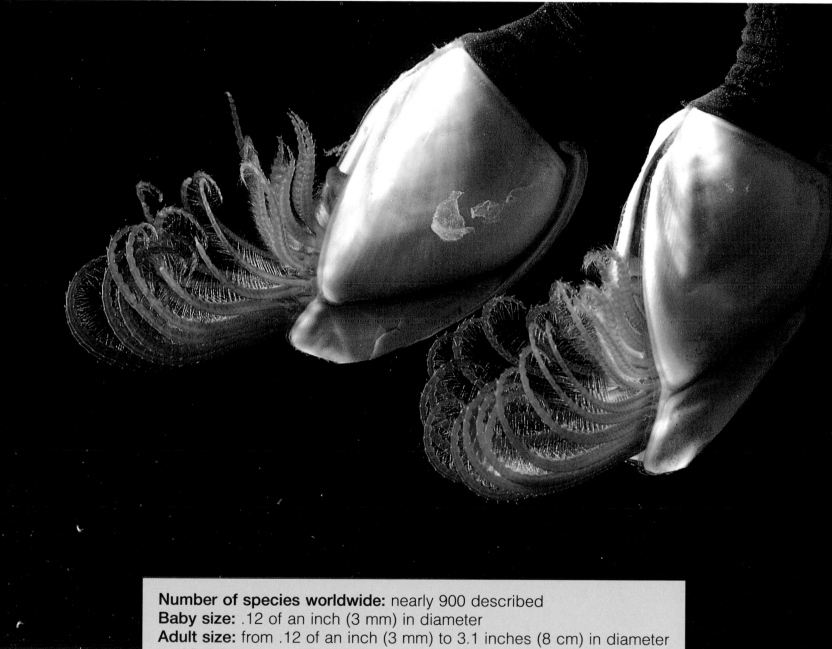

Number of species worldwide: nearly 900 described
Baby size: .12 of an inch (3 mm) in diameter
Adult size: from .12 of an inch (3 mm) to 3.1 inches (8 cm) in diameter and height of 9.1 inches (23 cm).
Where it lives: All species are saltwater animals that are either free-living or attach to objects such as rocks, shells, corals, wood boats, fishes, turtles, whales, and crabs.
Special features: Barnacle glue has been investigated for possible use in dentistry.

C

Cuttlefish (CUT-ul-fish)

Cuttlefish might well be called "cuddle" fish because they are so curious and responsive. They belong in the same family of *invertebrate* animals as the octopus and squid. Cuttlefish, like chameleons, can change colors instantaneously from rainbow colors to zebra stripes of brown and white. They use this ability in a colorful mating dance and to threaten or show alarm.

Cuttlefish young are born from eggs. Once the eggs are fertilized, the female chooses a place on a coral reef and glues large *egg capsules* there. The rubbery, elastic covering probably discourages predators, so the parents don't stay around to tend the eggs. Thirty to forty days later an animal that looks just like a miniature adult swims free of its egg capsule to pursue life on the reef. They often hide in the sand during the day, emerging to actively hunt at night.

Cuttlefish adult *(Sepia officinalis)* with tentacles raised

Cuttlefish *(Sepia officinalis)* eggs and newly hatched baby

Number of species worldwide: over 80
Baby size: *Sepia officinalis* hatchling, *.4 inches (12 mm)*
Adult size: depending on species from .6 to 19.7 inches (15 mm to 50 cm) long
Where it lives: most tropical and subtropical seas, especially in the Mediterranean, the Western Pacific, and the Indian Ocean
Special features: has ten arms, including two which are longer *tentacles,* which they shoot out to capture prey

D

Discus (DISK-us)

A freshwater fish from the Amazon River, the discus adds a new meaning to the expression "giving the shirt off your back." Both discus parents care for the eggs, which are laid on a rock or a leaf. Then each parent secretes a mucous slime over its entire body. When the babies emerge from the eggs, they are utterly dependent for the first few weeks of life, nibbling this mucous coat as their main source of food. Only when the babies are strong enough do they begin to feed on their own. And with their feeding services no longer required, parent discus slowly lose the special coating of extra slime.

Discus adults *(Symphysodon discus)*, with babies

Discus adults *(Symphysodon discus)* with another fish, the silver prochilodus (right)

Number of species worldwide: 2, including 5 subspecies
Baby size: around .16 of an inch (4 mm)
Adult size: 6–8 inches (15–20 cm)
Where it lives: in the Amazon River in South America
Special features: Both parents feed the young. They take turns by flicking their bodies to transfer the young to the other parent.

E

Eel

The North American eel tells one of the great water baby mystery stories of all time. Until the twentieth century, baby eels were thought to be a new species of fish. But when scientists discovered that the mystery fish was a migrating fish, they traced its route backwards from the adult breeding ground of the Sargasso Sea. Located in the Atlantic Ocean southwest of Bermuda off the eastern coast of the United States, the Sargasso Sea is the last stop for European and American eels. They die there after laying their eggs. A newly hatched eel baby looks like an odd, flat, transparent fish. It is called a leptocephalus, which means "slender or thin head."

As the leptocephalus drifts west with the Gulf Stream, it turns into a transparent *glass eel.* Somehow the European eels and the American eels know when to turn toward Europe or America. Though their arrival times are different, both kinds of eels then enter freshwater streams to live out most of the rest of their lives. Adult eels may wait twelve to twenty-four years before they start their final migration back to the Sargasso Sea. In the process, they have to go through lots of transformations. From a dark colored eel with small eyes, they develop the silvery body and enormous eyes of a deep-sea fish.

European eel *(Anguilla anguilla)* from northern Germany

Breeding-ground and distribution of European Freshwater and American Eels

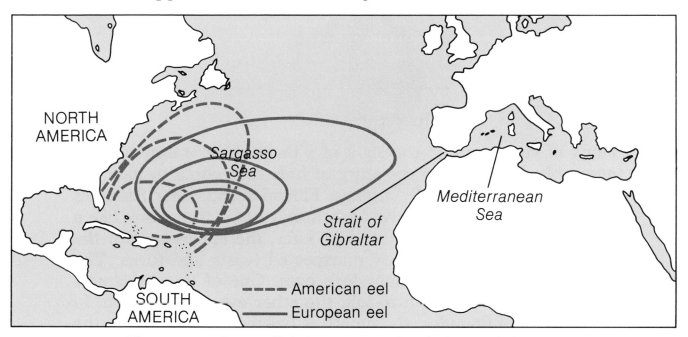

These young eels are called elvers, a stage after the leptocephalus stage

Number of species worldwide: freshwater eels, 16
Baby size: leptocephalus, about 2.4 inches (60 mm)
Adult size: larger female American eels, up to 5 feet (1.5 m)
Where it lives: freshwater inland, but returns to the sea to spawn
Special features: Fishermen catch eels with nets, hand lines, and traps as they are migrating downstream on their way to the sea.

E

Flounder (FLOWN-der)

Many of you may find the sight of a flounder on a dinner plate agreeably familiar. But the story of how they come to look the way they do is decidedly strange. Flounder and other flatfishes begin life as floating eggs. And when they hatch, they look like a lot of other fishes. But a few days later, the appearance of the flounder goes through a few unexpected twists and turns. The change begins with the flounder's eyes. One of them migrates over the back of the fish to join the other eye, side by side. In some kinds of flounder, the mouth is twisted, so it too faces the same direction as the two eyes.

The migration of the eye is the beginning of a new kind of life for the flounder. It will now spend the rest of its life swimming and lying on its eyeless side. Life on the bottom isn't so bad. Some kinds of flounder *camouflage* themselves by matching the color of the surrounding sand. In some species of flatfishes the eye migrates from the left side to the right. In others, the opposite occurs. Sometimes the same kind of flounder will have right-eyed and left-eyed fishes. Investigating why this happens may help us understand why some people are right- or left-handed.

Number of species worldwide: left-eye, 220; right-eye, 100
Baby size: Hatching larvae of some European flounders are .12 of an inch (3 mm) long.
Adult size: from a few inches (7.6 cm) to 10 feet (3 m) or more
Where it lives: throughout the tropical and temperate seas of the world
Special features: Flounder belong to a group of animals called flatfishes, which includes halibut, plaice, turbot, and sole, a group with over 600 described species.

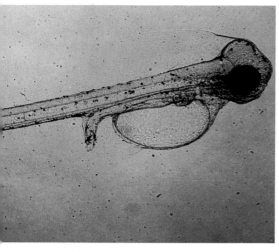

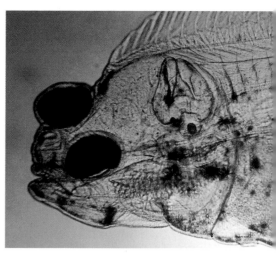

Three larval stages of the starry flounder *(Platichthys stellatus)*
showing migration of the eye from opposite sides of the fish to the same side.
This allows it to lie on the bottom and see with both its eyes.

F

15

G

Goosefish

The goosefish is better known as "monkfish," the name it is given in restaurants and markets. In Europe it is also called anglerfish, for a special fin it wiggles near its mouth like a fishing lure. The goosefish's mouth is so big, many fisherman call it the "all-mouth." Whatever you call it, with a gigantic head two-thirds its body length, the goosefish is a true sea monster. Lying camouflaged on the bottom of the ocean floor, it ambushes prey, which it gulps into its big Cheshire cat grin.

Baby goosefish look nothing like the adult, but they don't look like ordinary fishes either. They begin life as an immense veil of millions of eggs that float at the surface of the sea. A single goosefish ribbon of eggs may be over 30 feet (9 m) long. Once hatched, baby goosefish develop enormous pectoral or side fins, and long trailing fins sprout from the belly. Before they descend to live on the ocean floor, baby goosefish have already started to develop the adult's fringed and ghoulish smile.

Floating egg veil of the American goosefish
(*Lophius americanus*) which contains millions of eggs

Juvenile goosefish *(Lophius americanus)* swims with the plankton
until it undergoes metamorphosis and settles to a bottom-dwelling adult.

Adult American goosefish *(Lophius americanus)* showing its huge mouth and the sticklike lure that lies at
rest above its mouth

Number of species worldwide: 12, although the larger category of anglerfishes include 225 species
Baby size: American goosefish, .1 to 1.8 inches (2.5 to 4.5 mm) when hatched.
Adult size: American goosefish, up to 4 feet (1.2 m) long
Where it lives: bottom dwellers in all tropical and temperate marine waters of the world
Special features: The goosefish has been known to capture seabirds such as herring gulls, loons, and auks.

Female horseshoe crab *(Limulus polyphemus)* dragging the smaller male.
Males hold on until the female takes her fertilized eggs and buries them up out of water on the beach.

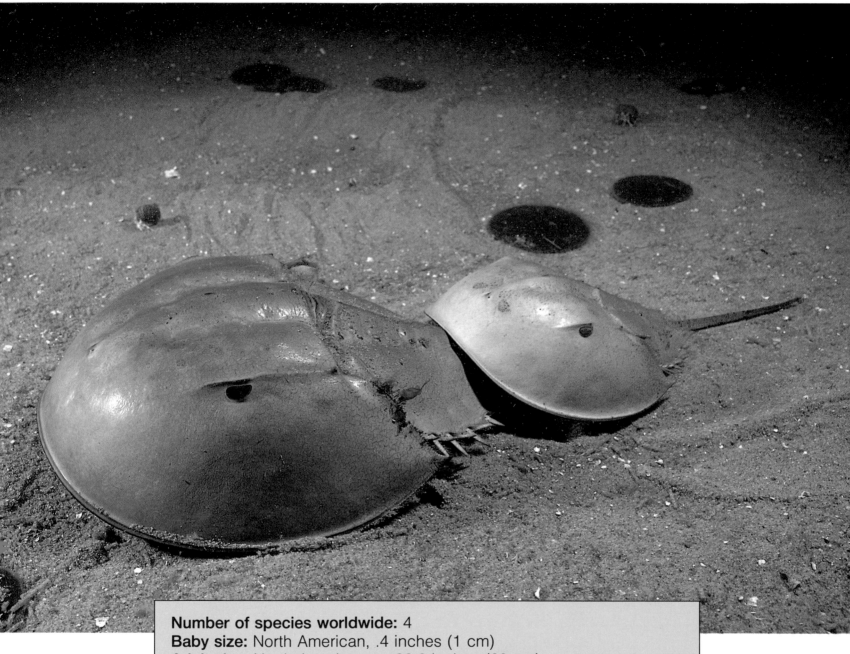

Number of species worldwide: 4
Baby size: North American, .4 inches (1 cm)
Adult size: North American, to 23.6 inches (60 cm)
Where it lives: North American horseshoe crabs live in shallow water on sandy or muddy shores; Gulf of Maine to the Gulf of Mexico.
Special features: Research on the horseshoe crab's eye has helped scientists understand human vision and the way our nerves work.

H

Horseshoe Crab

Horseshoe crab babies begin their life in the sand. Triggered by rising temperatures of spring and summer, mating pairs invade the beach in massive numbers. Males climb on top of the larger females for a ride up to the beach. The males have special hooks that allow them to hang on. Once sperm and egg are united, the female buries rubbery aquamarine clumps of eggs to wait for the rising tide. As the tide leaves, so do the crabs. After several weeks in the sand, eggs hatch into tiny larvae that look like undersea insects. But they don't become sexually mature until nine to twelve years later.

Horseshoe crab blood has given scientists an important weapon in the fight against infection in humans. Substances in the blood can help doctors detect signs of diseases such as spinal meningitis (SPINE-ul men-in-JITE-us). Understanding the secrets of horseshoe crab birth may eventually assure the preservation of this unique animal as well as save human lives.

Baby horseshoe crabs *(Limulus polyphemus)* still protected by their egg capsules

I

Insects

A scientist in the rain forest once came up with a clever idea to collect insects from the treetops where most animals reside. Instead of climbing 130 feet (39.6 meters), he directed a cloud of insect-killing smoke up into the forest canopy and then collected all the bugs that fell into a waiting net. As the result of this experiment, he estimated the number of insects that tropical treetops could hold to be between 10 and 30 million. Insects—and that includes insects that live part of their lives in water—outnumber the rest of the animal world by astonishing numbers.

Insects like the *water boatman,* the *water strider,* and the *whirligig beetle* spend their lives in the water. But many insects spend only their early life stages there. This sometimes requires special means to survive. Mosquito babies live in the water almost anywhere. They survive not because of gills, but because they can breathe oxygen from the air with a snorkel-like tube in their tail. Thanks to their life in the water, mosquitoes can then fly off to torment mammals like ourselves.

Larva of these mosquitoes use built-in snorkels to breathe air at the surface of the water.

A young mosquito *(Culex pipiens)* emerges from the water.

An adult water strider (family *Gerridae*) uses its slender legs to walk across the surface of the water.

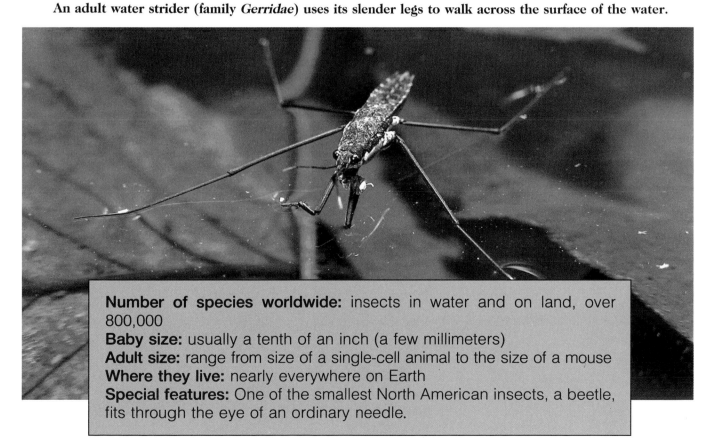

Number of species worldwide: insects in water and on land, over 800,000

Baby size: usually a tenth of an inch (a few millimeters)

Adult size: range from size of a single-cell animal to the size of a mouse

Where they live: nearly everywhere on Earth

Special features: One of the smallest North American insects, a beetle, fits through the eye of an ordinary needle.

J

Jacana (ju-KAN-uh)

The jacana is a water bird that sometimes gets only its feet wet. These tropical freshwater birds have such long toes and claws they seem to be able to walk on water. Actually, they step from leaf to leaf of floating water plants. Jacanas build nests of plant debris that form rafts on top of the water. Inside they lay four eggs which hatch a little over three weeks later. Unlike penguin chicks whose down coat is not waterproof, jacana chicks come equipped with a camouflaged feather suit that enables them to swim and dive immediately.

With the American jacana, it's the female that has the last say. After she lays her eggs, the male is the one that tends the eggs. This leaves the female free to bond with yet another male and produce additional clutches of eggs.

An adult African jacana *(Actophilornis africana)* shelters its chick.

The Northern jacana *(Jacana spinosa)* from Costa Rica, Central America, uses long, slender legs to walk across lily pads.

Number of species worldwide: 8
Egg size: average 1.2 inches (30.1 mm)
Adult size: 10–13 inches (25.4–33 cm)
Where it lives: tropical lakes and rivers of Africa, India, Asia, Australia, Central and South America
Special features: Also called the Jesus Christ bird by South American natives for its ability to "walk on water"

Mummichogs *(Fundulus heteroclitus)* are one of the many kinds of killifishes worldwide.

Number of species worldwide: over 400 in the family *Cyprinodontidae*
Baby size: killifish called a mummichog, .28 inches (7 mm) larvae at hatching
Adult size: 1.5–7 inches (3.8–17.8 cm), depending on species
Where it lives: widespread in all temperate and tropical waters of the world, along the coasts, not in open water
Special features: noteworthy for tolerance of extreme temperatures, salinities, and lack of water

K

Killifish (KIL-i-fish)

Imagine giving birth in a footprint or the rut left by the tire of a passing car. That's what some remarkable little killifish are able to do. They are masters of the instant baby. If water doesn't stay around long enough for their eggs to hatch right away, the eggs simply dry up, and may even blow away to land in a wetter place. Typically, killifish come out when the rains come, live for a few weeks, lay eggs, and then die. The mummichog, a common ocean killifish, often lays its eggs in very shallow water in mussel shells, so when the tide goes out, the mussel shell cradles the eggs and some water. This protects the eggs from predators long enough to hatch and swim away with an incoming tide.

An embryo of a killifish *(Fundulus sp.)* develops inside its egg capsule.

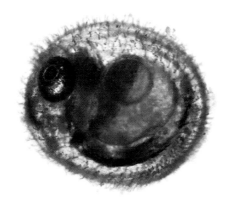

L

Lobster

A lobster baby begins life as one of 5,000 to 100,000 eggs attached under the curve of a female lobster's tail. And it's this kind of protection that helps assure the survival of a female lobster's young at least in this beginning stage. But once she has carried the eggs for up to a year, she shakes her tiny babies free to float to the surface. There they remain, prey to birds and animals of the sea until they have developed enough to sink back to the ocean floor. This drifting stage may last a month or slightly more.

Lobsters can be reared in captivity, but it is a long and difficult process. The main problem with captive rearing is that young lobsters eat other young lobsters.

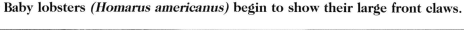

Baby lobsters _(Homarus americanus)_ begin to show their large front claws.

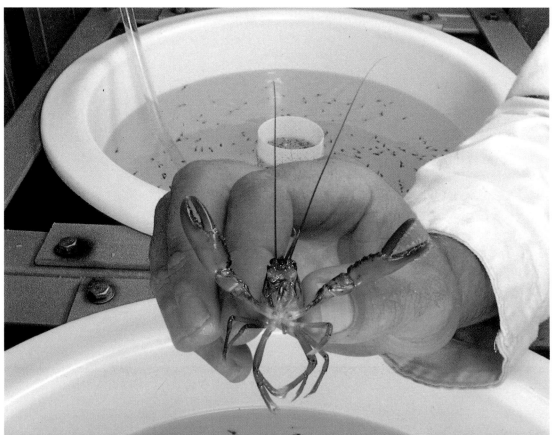

A female lobster *(Homarus americanus)* holds her clutch of eggs on the underside of her tail.

Number of species worldwide: 163, including clawed and spiny lobsters

Baby size: American lobster, .33 inch (8 mm)

Adult size: American lobster, to 23.6 inches (60 cm)

Where it lives: The American lobster lives on rocky ocean bottoms in holes and crevices.

Special features: Spiny lobsters, the tropical cousins of the American lobsters, don't have the large delicious front claws.

M

Mola mola (MOLE-ah MOLE-ah)

Spotting a mola mola in the open sea is rather like encountering a creature from another planet. Mola molas are also called ocean sunfishes because they are often found floating on the surface as if they were sunning themselves. The mola mola's scaleless, leathery, and slimy skin encloses an immense oval-shaped body up to 11 feet (4 meters) long. Its top and bottom fins look like the giant keels of an oceangoing sailboat. Viewed fom the side, it appears to be a fish with its tail bitten off.

Don't let the mola mola's awkward appearance deceive you. They swim powerfully and fast, from the surface of the ocean down to a thousand feet or more. Along the way they feast on everything from jelly animals called sea acorns to baby fishes and invertebrates.

If you think the adult is odd-looking, wait until you see mola mola babies. Hatched from millions of floating eggs, ocean sunfish babies begin life in the shape of pincushions or balls of thorns. They may not win any beauty awards, but their spines scare most predators off. When they are about an inch long, babies begin to develop fins that resemble the fins of their parents.

The pincushion-like mola mola *(Mola mola)* larva looks very little like the adult.

Adult ocean sunfish *(Mola mola)* **with diver**

Number of molas worldwide: 3
Baby size: .12 inch (3 mm)
Adult size: to 10 feet (3 m) long, 11 feet (3.3 m) high from top-most to bottom-most fins
Where it lives: Offshore tropical and temperate waters of the world
Special features: Mola molas have been kept in public aquariums on a diet of shrimp.

N

Nudibranch (NOOD-uh-brank)

Also called a sea slug, the nudibranch's breathtaking colors make it the butterfly of the ocean. Like the butterfly, nudibranch babies are born in a form and shape that changes through metamorphosis. First the parent produces jelly-coated ribbons of thousands of eggs. The egg develops into what looks like a snail with a shell like a *periwinkle*. Nudibranchs are closely related to snails.

At the snail-shell stage, the babies are called *veligers*. Soon they break free of their bed of jelly to float in the ocean's currents. But once the veliger finds a special food it will eat as an adult, it settles, loses its shell, uncurls its body, and becomes a tiny adult. Some nudibranches grow to young adulthood without ever leaving the jelly ribbon. But most flatten up on tiny, single-celled plants in the ocean before they lose their shell.

Number of species worldwide: over 2,500
Baby size: some larval shells are .01–.02 inches (.28–.30 mm)
Adult size: from .08–7.9 inches (2–200 mm)
Where it lives: all the world's oceans and major seas
Special features: Some species eat the stinging cells of the tentacles of invertebrate animals called anemones and hydroids and transfer them to tentacles on their own backs.

The larval stage of nudibranchs called veligers still show a shell, which they will later lose through metamorphosis.

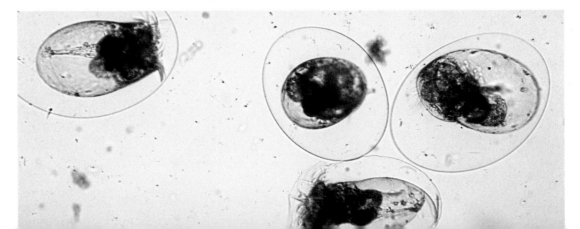

A nudibranch (shell-less snail) adult *(Coryphella* sp*)* crawls near recently laid strips of eggs.

A speckled sea lemon nudibranch *(Anisodoris nobilis)* lays its eggs in the cold waters off British Columbia, Canada.

Adult octopus (*Octopus joubini*)

Number of species worldwide: over 150
Baby size: as small as .08 inch (2 mm)
Adult size: Largest octopus species, *Octopus doefleini,* can measure 30 feet (9.1 m) across with its tentacles spread out.
Where it lives: Octopuses live in nearly all the seas of the world from the tropics to the Arctic and Antarctic.
Special features: The common octopus can lay as many as 150,000 or more eggs at a time.

Octopus (AHK-ta-puss)

Relatives of squid and cuttlefish, some octopuses are so intelligent they can learn to unscrew the top of a glass jar to get a tasty crab inside. The octopus mother and father have an unconventional courtship. The male passes a "packet" of sperm to its mate with a special modified arm. Octopus babies appear first as strings of eggs that the female hangs at the top of the cave where she lives. The mother keeps a close watch. She cleans the eggs with her tentacles and squirts jets of water on them to make sure they get enough oxygen. The mothers of all octopuses die after their young swim free.

The developing eggs of *Octopus joubini* show tiny octopus miniatures inside.

The developing egg of *Octopus joubini* shows a tiny octopus miniature inside.

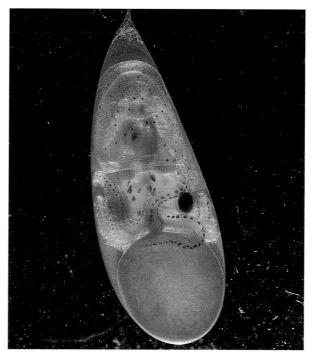

P

Penguin (PEN-gwen)

Penguins are birds that do their "flying" underwater. As with other birds, baby penguins are born from eggs. Some penguins, such as the blackfooted penguins of South Africa, produce two equal-sized eggs a few days apart. Others, such as the rockhoppers, lay two different-sized eggs. Inside the egg, the developing *embryo* feeds on a built-in food supply called a *yolk sac*.

Once the eggs have hatched, parent penguins pass food from their own mouths into the beaks of their young. Chicks develop a downy coat to keep them warm. Despite this down, they also depend on their parents' special "brood patches," folds in the parent's belly that shield the chicks from the cold. Down absorbs water and would make the baby birds waterlogged, so the young penguins do not swim until they lose their first coat. They eat so ravenously, though, that as soon as a month after birth, they triple their size, lose their down, and take on a juvenile's oily, streamlined feathers similar to the adult's.

Eggs of blackfooted *(Spheniscus demersus)* and rockhopper *(Eudyptes crestatus)* penguins inside an incubator to help them develop

Juvenile blackfooted penguins *(Spheniscus demersus)* have a coat of baby down, which they lose as they mature.

Jackass penguins *(Spheniscus demersus)* in a colony off South Africa

Number of species worldwide: 17
Baby size: blackfooted penguins, about 3 inches (7.6 cm) long
Adult size: blackfooted penguins, 12–18 inches (30.5–45.7 cm) tall
Where it lives: West coast of Africa, ranging up into the tropics. There are at least 18 species of penguins worldwide that live from the Antarctic to South America and South Africa.
Special features: Blackfooted penguins provide many generations of penguins for the public to see in zoos and aquariums by reproducing in special facilities away from the wild.

Q

Quahog (KO-hog)

The common chowder clam called a quahog begins life after male and female adults release clouds of sperm and eggs into the surrounding water. The fertilized eggs then go through cell division and through several developmental stages until they swim off the bottom as curious-looking veligers. A veliger looks a little like a miniature clam, but at one end it has a set of fleshy lips covered with tiny, beating *cilia* or hairs. Called a *velum,* this cilia-lined structure lets the baby quahog swim up and down in the water to feed on tiny plants.

Beginning in this veliger stage the baby clam starts to develop the hard shell it will have as an adult. A long foot begins to form, and the youngster, now called a pediveliger (*pedi* means "foot") starts to spend more time on the bottom looking for a place to settle. When it has found a good place, the veliger absorbs its swimming organ, the velum, and changes (through metamorphosis) into a miniature adult.

Number of species worldwide: over 8,000 species of bivalves, which include clams, mussels, and scallops
Baby size: *Mercenaria mercenaria,* less than half an inch (1 mm)
Adult size: *Mercenaria mercenaria,* to 5 inches (12.7 cm)
Where it lives: (*Mercenaria mercenaria*), from the Gulf of St. Lawrence to Florida and Texas, introduced into California
Special features: The name quahog comes from Indian words meaning "closed shell."

The larval stage

Adult quahog (Mercenaria mercenaria)

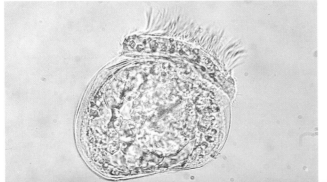

R

Rotifer (ROTE-if-er)

Although there are close to 2,000 kinds of rotifers in the fresh and salt waters of the world, rotifers are among the least familiar water animals because they are so small. Most are less than .04 inch (.1 cm). They are called wheel animals because of the crown of rapidly beating hairs or cilia they use to get around and to sweep food into their mouths. Some kinds of rotifers live solitary lives carried in water currents, others live in groups attached to a surface like a rock.

Some baby rotifers are produced by male and female parents. But others are the result of parthenogenesis (parth-en-no-JEN-ah-sis), a process in which a baby is produced from an egg even though no sperm has fertilized the egg. Some rotifer eggs are able to go into hibernation or dormancy. They can stay that way for months and then spring back to life when conditions allow.

Rotifers play a vital role in *aquaculture*. If fishes are raised and farmed in special aquariums away from their natural environment, food has to be supplied to help them grow. Rotifers are small enough to fit in the mouth of many fish babies, and thus provide a ready supply of food that allows baby fishes to grow.

Number of species worldwide: over 2,000
Baby size: microscopic
Adult size: may reach .12 inches (3 mm)
Where it lives: throughout the world in fresh water and salt, and even on land, associated with mosses and lichens when they are filled with water
Special features: Some rotifers can dry up and remain in a dormant state for up to four years and then become active again.

The rotifer uses the cilia, or hairs, around its mouth to move about and capture food.

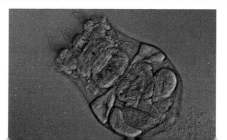

S

Shark

A little more than 100 of the 350 or so kinds of sharks lay eggs. The rest give birth to live sharks that are born anywhere from a few months to a few years after the egg is fertilized. The sand tiger and the horn sharks tell two of the strangest baby shark stories. Like all sharks, sand tiger mothers have two *uteri* for their developing young. But in each uterus, the first baby shark to develop eats either the eggs or their brothers or sisters just after they have hatched. This sort of shark cannibalism helps the two surviving babies get ready for life on their own.

The horn shark gets its name from the two spinelike fins on its back. Horn shark babies begin life in an egg capsule that looks like the bit of a huge drill. Once placed by its mother in a rocky hideaway, the spiraled capsule is nearly impossible for a predator to pull free. Inside, a horn shark embryo lives on its yolk sac for nearly a year until it is ready to swim free.

An adult sand tiger shark (*Odontaspis taurus*)

A shiner perch glides past the odd-looking egg (above) of a hornshark adult *(Heterodontus francisci)* pictured (below). Its drill-like egg case makes it easier to lodge in a rock crevice to ensure its safety.

Number of species worldwide: over 350
Baby size: one-week-old sand tiger, 3.3 feet (1 m) long
Adult size: sand tiger, up to 10 feet (3 m) long
Where it lives: Atlantic waters off European and North American coasts
Special features: Medical researchers are very interested in sharks because sharks have amazing resistance to diseases.

A leatherback turtle *(Dermochelys coriacea)* lays its eggs in the sand and then buries them for safety.

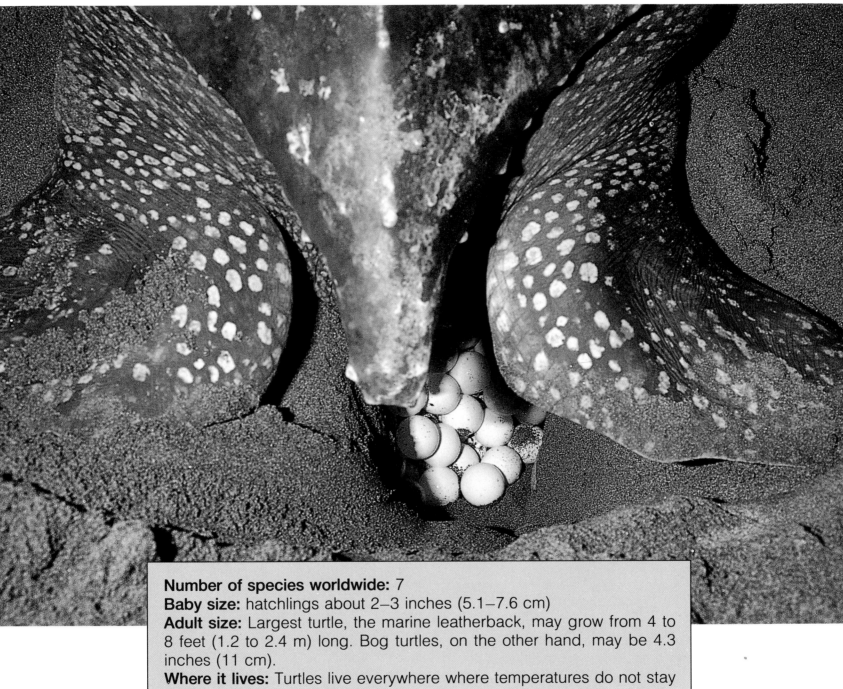

Number of species worldwide: 7
Baby size: hatchlings about 2–3 inches (5.1–7.6 cm)
Adult size: Largest turtle, the marine leatherback, may grow from 4 to 8 feet (1.2 to 2.4 m) long. Bog turtles, on the other hand, may be 4.3 inches (11 cm).
Where it lives: Turtles live everywhere where temperatures do not stay cold throughout the year: on land and in the sea, in deserts, forests, and grasslands.
Special features: All seven or more species of sea turtles are endangered.

T

Turtle (TERT-ul)

Turtles live throughout the world as long as temperatures don't get too cold. They are especially abundant in warm seas, hot southern swamps, and jungle rivers. Turtles produce babies by laying eggs, often after mighty courtship battles among males for the female of their choice. Most female turtles lay from two to twenty eggs at a time, although big sea turtles can produce eggs in the hundreds. Aquatic turtles come out of the water to dig pits in the sand to bury their eggs. Once the mother has hidden her eggs, she leaves them to develop on their own. How long turtle eggs take to hatch depends on the warmth of the soil. But once the egg development is finished, the young use a sharp *egg tooth* to break their way to freedom. They look like miniature versions of the adult.

Burying eggs on a beach provides incubation and protection from predators in the sea. But it is also the reason so many turtles are endangered. Atlantic Ridley turtles, for example, migrate thousands of miles each year to the same Mexican beach. People who hunt eggs to sell them at market take advantage of the turtles' predictable behavior. The price for the turtle may soon be extinction.

Loggerhead turtle *(Caretta caretta)* babies emerge from the sand and quickly head for the sea.

U

Urchin (IR-chun)

Before the sea urchin baby matures, it looks more like an underwater spaceship than the pincushion adult that grazes on the ocean floor. Sea urchins cast sperm and eggs into the ocean where they unite to form thousands of young. As few as twelve hours later, eggs become babies that look like upside-down umbrellas. At this stage, babies are called larvae and they are not quite as helpless as they may look. Their long arms are stiffened by a calcium skeleton, and they are lined with tiny cilia, or hairs that help keep them afloat. Sea urchin larvae feed on tiny floating plants for as long as several months. Sensing it's time for a change, larvae sink to the bottom and quickly—in as little as an hour's time—change from a spaceship shape to a spiny ball.

Baby sea urchins and brittle stars look like spaceships and they are well designed to float in the ocean.

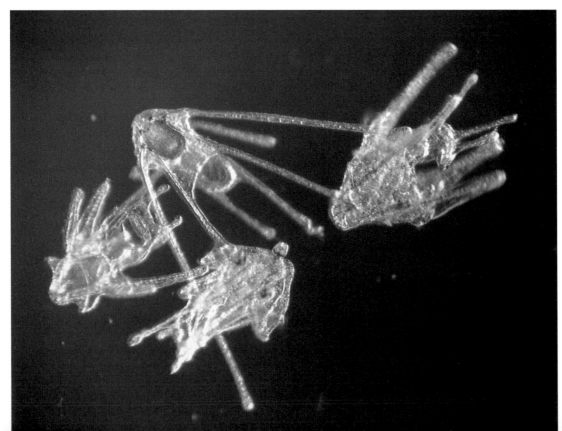

Number of species worldwide: about 950 species of echinoids: sea urchins, heart urchins, and sand dollars
Baby size: less than half an inch (1.3 cm)
Adult size: most are 2.4–4.7 inches (6–12 cm) in diameter, some up to 14.2 inches (36 cm)
Where it lives: coastal areas in rocky depressions, tropical reefs, and on sandy bottoms
Special features: Some sea urchin eggs are considered a delicacy like caviar.

V

Velella (vel-LEL-lah) or By-the-Wind-Sailor

A relative of the jellyfish and anemone, the *Velella* is like an oval jelly raft topped off with a structure that looks like a sail. And sail it does, blown by the wind as it floats along the surface of the sea. A curtain of stinging polyps, or tentacles, hangs from the *Velella*. These capture tiny shrimp and other animals floating in the *plankton*.

Besides the feeding tentacles, *Velella* also dangle other polyps that are used for reproduction. They produce *buds,* miniature male and female jellyfishlike creatures, that gradually sink to the bottom of the sea. Budding is called asexual reproduction because it's done by cell division, not by the union of sperm and eggs. But now it's the buds' turn to reproduce. From their fertilized eggs come *Velella* larvae, animals that then come to resemble the adult and float to the surface of the sea.

Number of species worldwide: about 10 closely related species
Baby size: .39 inches (1 cm) and smaller
Adult size: .2–3 inches (.5–7.5 cm) in diameter
Where it lives: open sea in tropical and temperate zones
Special features: average *Velella* has a 2-inch (5.1 cm) sail

**By-the-wind sailors *(Velella velella)* use their
sails to get around on the surface of the ocean.**

W

Whales

You may have trouble thinking of a 22-foot (6.7 meters) long animal as a baby, but that is the size of a baby blue whale at birth. Perhaps the 15-foot (4.5 meters) long humpback or the 5–6 foot long (1.5 to 1.8 meters) longfin pilot whale seem more babylike to you. As mammals like you and me, whale mothers give birth to live young, almost always a single baby. After nine to eighteen months of development inside the mother, whale babies, called calves, are usually born tail first. They are carefully protected by the mother during the first weeks of life. Depending on whether a whale is a *toothed whale* or a *baleen* whale, nursing can go on for four months to several years.

Once born, whales don't waste any time putting on weight. In the seven months a blue whale feeds on its mother's fat-rich milk, it gains over 170 pounds (77 kilograms) a day. A blue whale may double its length by the time it has reached the age of two.

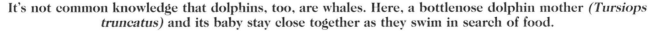

It's not common knowledge that dolphins, too, are whales. Here, a bottlenose dolphin mother *(Tursiops truncatus)* and its baby stay close together as they swim in search of food.

A killer whale *(Orcinus orca)* and its baby swim in the shallows.

Number of species worldwide: 67 toothed whales, 10 baleen whales
Baby size: blue whale, 22 feet (6.7 m); fin whale, 21.3 feet (6.5 meters); humpback, 15 feet (4.5 m); longfin pilot whale, 5.9 feet (1.8m)
Adult size: blue whale 50+ feet (15.2 m); humpback 48 feet (14.6 m)
Where it lives: all oceans and some fresh waters
Special features: The most endangered large whale is the North Atlantic right whale; there may be fewer than 300 of these animals left.

X

Xenopus (ZEEN-ah-puss) or African Clawed Frog

Xenopus (ZEEN-ah-puss) or African Clawed Frog

Xenopus is the scientific name for the African clawed frog. Frog babies are familiar to many of us because of the many tadpoles we can find in city and country ponds and streams. The African clawed frog is a bit strange, though. It starts life as a transparent egg, then becomes an almost completely transparent tadpole which swims around in mid-water and eats plankton. In about two months it becomes a frog.

After metamorphosis from a tadpole to a juvenile frog, *Xenopus* become ravenous hunters that will eat just about anything they can catch. They are also an example of the bad things that can happen when an animal is taken from its original home and introduced somewhere else. *Xenopus* are popular and appealing to home aquarists as little froglets, but they soon grow large and jump at anything that moves. Some that were released in southern California now threaten small native fishes and tadpoles in the California streams.

Xenopus tadpole *(Xenopus laevis)*

The African clawed frog *(Xenopus laevis)* uses its webbed feet to scurry underwater and to swim to the surface to breathe.

Number of species worldwide: over 6
Baby size: *Xenopus laevis* tadpole, .5 inches (1.3 cm) egg .39 inches (1 cm)
Adult size: *Xenopus laevis* to 5 inches (12.7 cm) or more
Where it lives: Native range is central and southern Africa but they have been introduced to lots of other places
Special features: A female *Xenopus* can produce as many as 15,000 eggs in a single year.

Y

Yellowfin Tuna

From eggs the size of pinheads, baby tuna fish emerge just two days after the eggs are laid. They start eating almost immediately. Only an eighth of an inch long, newly hatched tuna look like little monsters with huge heads and big teeth. They'll hunt anything small enough to fit in their mouths, including zooplankton, and soon even tiny fish. Given their enormous appetites, it's not surprising that tuna grow very fast. Yellowfin tuna can gain up to 60 pounds (27.2 kg) in one year.

Yellowfins often end up as canned tuna. Unfortunately, in some places the nets they're caught in catch dolphins as well. For reasons not yet clear, dolphins swim in groups above yellowfin schools in the Pacific Ocean. When fishermen use their nets to catch yellowfin, they also injure or kill dolphins. Public concern over the fate of dolphins has even persuaded some packagers of canned tuna to stop buying the yellowfin variety, until fishing techniques change.

Number of species of tuna and mackerel: 47
Baby size: yellowfin tuna, .15 inch (4mm)
Adult size: yellowfin tuna, up to 6.8 feet (2.1 m) long, up to 400 pounds (182 kg)
Where it lives: tropical and warm temperate seas
Special features: The yellowfish tuna's large cousin, the bluefish, may reach 14 feet (4.3 m) and 1,500 pounds (680kg).

The tapered shape of these yellowfin tuna *(Thunnus albacares)* means they are designed for maximum underwater speed.

Z

Zooplankton (zoh-ah-PLANK-ton)

Zooplankton is a mixture of tiny animals. Some are adults of small creatures and others are the babies of larger ones. These water babies of what later become larger animals drift about in the water for part of their lives.

Zooplankton form the diet of countless water animals. Animals as large as a mighty 50-foot (15.2 m) whale scoop up zooplankton in the millions as their exclusive source of food. See if you can guess what each of the zooplankton babies pictured on the facing page will grow up to look like as an adult.

Larva of crab, Great Barrier Reef, Australia

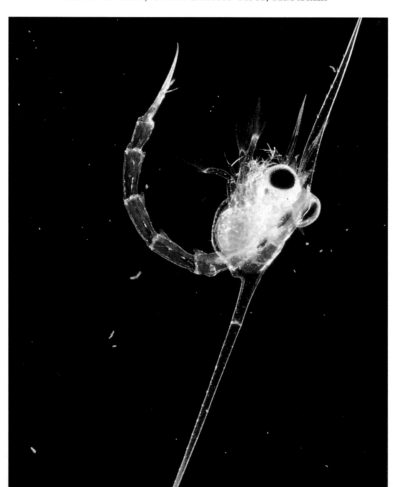

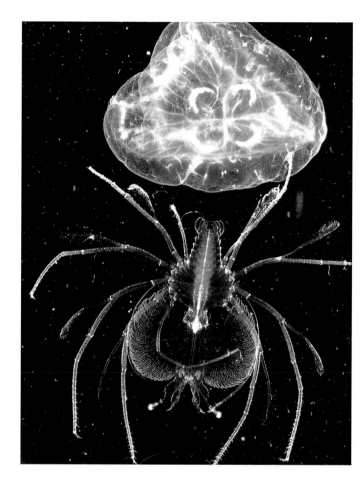

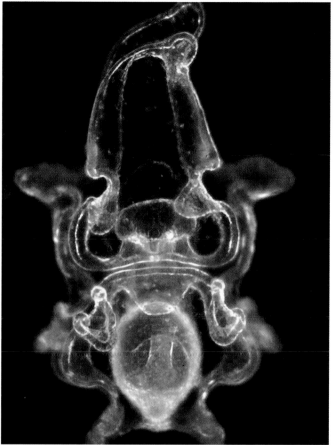

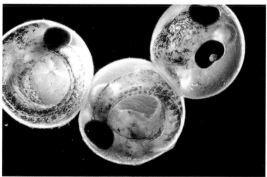

Adult size: up to 2 inches (50 mm) or more
Where it lives: fresh and salt water
Special features: Seventy percent of the invertebrates that live on the ocean floor become zooplankton during part of their life cycle.

$$\frac{\mathbf{Z}}{51}$$

GLOSSARY

aquaculture (AK-wa KULT-chur)—the cultivation of fish, shellfish, and aquatic plants

baleen whale (buh-LEEN)—whale that catches fishes and plankton from the sea using a filter made of strips of hard, flexible material called baleen that hang from the upper jaw. Humpbacks and blue whales are baleen whales.

buds—outgrowths of an organism that develop into new individuals

calcium skeleton (CAL-see-um SKELL-ut-ton)—Body structure, made of calcium compounds, that provides support

camouflage (KAM-ah-flaj)—to hide or disguise oneself by blending body color, texture, or shape into the background

cilia (SILL-ee-ah)—tiny, short, hairlike structures that help an organism swim or feed by beating back and forth

egg capsule—a protective case that encloses an egg or eggs

egg tooth—a hard, sharp bump on the beak of an unhatched bird, or the nose of an unhatched reptile, used to break open the eggshell. It usually disappears shortly after hatching.

embryo (EM-bree-oh)—a vertebrate in the early stages of growth before birth or hatching

extinction (ek-STINK-shun)—the complete disappearance of a species of living organism

glass eel—young, transparent life stage of the common eel

invertebrate (in-VERT-ah-brate)—animal without a backbone, such as a jellyfish, lobster, or an insect

larva (LAR-va), plural larvae (LAR-vee)—early form of an animal that does not resemble the adult form

mammal (MAM-ul)—any of a group of vertebrates, including humans, that have hair and nourish their young with milk from mammary glands

metamorphosis (met-uh-MORE-fah-sis)—a striking change in the form of an animal as it develops after birth or hatching

pectoral fin (PECK-tuh-rul)—one of a pair of fins usually located on the sides of a fish's body behind the gill covers

periwinkle (PER-i-win-kul)—any of various snails common in salt marshes and rocky sea shores

polyp (POL-up)—a stage in the lives of jellyfishes, sea anemones, and corals consisting of a simple stomach with a mouth surrounded by tentacles

plankton (PLANK-ton)—free-floating, often microscopic plants or animals that live in water and that usually depend on water currents to move them around

predators (PRED-at-ors)—animals and sometimes plants that eat other animals

rockhopper penguin—small penguin with yellow crest feathers and red, beady eyes, found all over the southern hemisphere in cool-temperature regions

species (SPEE-sheez)—scientific term for a group of individuals that can and do interbreed and produce fertile offspring in the wild

tadpole—the larva, usually aquatic and fish-like, of a frog or toad

tentacles—long, flexible structures, usually on an animal's head or around its mouth, used for grasping or stinging

toothed whale—a whale that captures food with teeth instead of baleen

uterus—a hollow organ of female mammals where an egg is deposited and an embryo develops

veliger (VEE-luh-jer)—larva of invertebrate animals, such as snails and clams, which has a shell and stays afloat by beating its cilia

velum (VEH-lum)—swimming organ of the veliger larva of animals such as snails and clams

venom (VEN-um)—poisonous substance that some animals transmit to enemies or prey by biting or stinging

water boatman—water insect with large hind legs used for rowing through the water

water strider—water insect that uses its thin legs to skate across the surface of the water

whirligig beetle (HWUR-li-gig BEET-ul)—water insect that often whirls in circles on the water surface

womb (WOOM)—an organ in the female animal for containing and nourishing the young before birth

yolk (YOKE)—the thick, usually golden yellow material that provides food for a very young animal

yolk sac—a sac containing food (yolk) that is attached to an animal developing in an egg

BIBLIOGRAPHY

1. The material on fishes is developed from Bigelow and Schroeder, *Fishes of the Gulf of Maine* (Washington D.C.: United States Government Printing Office, 1953); Q. Bone and N.B. Marshall, illustrated by Q. Bone, *Biology of Fishes* (New York: Distributed in the United States by Routledge, Chapman and Hall, 1982); Maurice Burton, *The New Larousse Encyclopedia of Animal Life* (New York: Bonanza Books, 1967); E. Clark, *The Lady and the Sharks* (New York: Harper and Row, 1969); E. Clark, "Sharks: Magnificent and Misunderstood," Washington D.C. National Geographic Magazine, vol. 160, no. 2, August 1981) 142–186; Joanna Cole, *A Fish Hatches* (New York: William Morrow and Company, 1978); B. Curtis, *The Life Story of the Fish: His Manners and Morals* (New York: Dover Publications, Inc., 1961); G. Fryer and T. Iles, *The Cichlid Fishes of the Great Lakes of Africa* (Neptune, N.J.: T.F.H. Publications, Inc., 1972); Michael Goulding, *The Fishes and the Forest* (Berkeley, Calif.: University of California Press, 1980) 210–1; Earl Herald, *Fishes of North America* (New York: Doubleday and Company, Inc.); Lagler, Bardach, Miller, Passino, *Ichthyology 2nd Edition* (New York: John Wiley & Sons, 1977); J.R. Norman, *A History of Fishes* (London: Ernest Benn Limited, 1975; Third Edition by P.H. Greenwood); Dorothy Patent, *Fish and How They Reproduce* (New York: Holiday House, 1976)

58–60, 70–75, 86–89, 90–95; Gunther Sterba, *Freshwater Fishes of the World* (New York: The Pet Library, 1967); Ronald E. Thresher, *Reef Fish* (Columbia, S.C.: The Palmetto Publishing Company, 1980) 131–136; and Alwyne Wheeler, *Fishes of the World* (New York: Macmillan Publishing Co., Inc., 1975).

2. The material on invertebrates is developed from Keith Banister and Andrew Campbell, *The Illustrated Encyclopedia of Aquatic Life* (New York: Facts on File, 1985); Peter Farb and The Editors of LIFE, *The Insects* (New York: Time Incorporated, 1962) 141–159; Kenneth Gosner, *A Field Guide to the Atlantic Seashore—The Peterson Guide Series* (Boston: Houghton Mifflin, 1978); B. Grzimek, *Grzimek's Animal Life Encyclopedia, Volume 1, Lower Animals* (New York: Van Nostrand Reinhold Company, 1972) 142–3, 195–6; M. Jacobson and D. Franz, *Wonders of Corals and Coral Reefs* (New York: Dodd, Mead & Company, 1979) 14–38; Lorus and Margery Milne, *Invertebrates of North America* (New York: Doubleday and Company, Inc.); Kaye Mash, *How Invertebrates Live* (London: Elsevier–Phaidon, 1975) 101–115; A. Ross and W. Emerson, *Wonders of Barnacles* (New York: Dodd, Mead & Company, 1974) 18–21, 22–37; T.E. Thompson, *Nudibranchs* (Neptune, N.J.: T.F.H. Publications, Inc., 1976) 79–86; and Warren Zeiller, *Tropical Marine Invertebrates of Southern Florida and the Bahama Islands* (New York: John Wiley and Sons, 1974) 26.

3. The material on mammals is developed from John Farrand, Jr. *The Audubon Society Encyclopedia of Animal Life* (New York: Clarkson N. Potter, Inc., 1982); Sir Richard Harrison and M.M. Bryden, *Whales, Dolphins, and Porpoises* (New York, Oxford, England: Facts on File Publications, 1988); Katona, Rough, Richardson, *A Field Guide to the Whales, Porpoises, and Seals of the Gulf of Maine and Eastern Canada* (New York: Charles Scribner's Sons, 1983); Kenneth Mallory and Andrea Conley, *Rescue of the Stranded Whales* (New York: Simon and Schuster, 1989); L. Harrison Matthews, *The Natural History of the Whale,* (New York: Columbia University Press, 1978); and Everhard J. Slijper, Whales and Dolphins (Ann Arbor, Mich.: The University of Michigan Press, 1977).

4. The material on amphibians is developed from B. Grzimek, *Grzimek's Animal Life Encyclopedia, Volume 5, Fishes II and Amphibians* (New York: Van Nostrand Reinbhold Company, 1974), 386.

5. The material on reptiles is developed from Ada and Frank Graham, *Alligators: An Audubon Reader* (New York: Delacorte Press, 1979); and B. Grzimek, *Grzimek's Animal Life Encyclopedia, Volume 6, Reptiles* (New York; Van Nostrand Reinhold Company, 1975), 75–123, 124–146.

6. The material on birds is developed from B. Grzimek, *Grzimek's Animal Life Encyclopedia, Volume 8, Birds II* (New York: Van Nostrand Reinhold Company, 1975), 144–6; and G. Simpson, *Penguins: Past and Present, Here and There* (New Haven and London: Yale University Press, 1976) 77–117.

7. Notes on the conservation of aquatic animals are taken from J. Cousteau and staff of the Cousteau Society, *The Cousteau Almanac* (New York: Doubleday & Company, Inc., 1981); Lee Durrell, *State of the Ark* (New York: Doubleday and Company, Inc., 1986); and Les Kaufman and Kenneth Mallory, *The Last Extinction* (Cambridge, Mass.: The MIT Press, 1986).

INDEX